DELIVERANCE

Maiche Lev

DELIVERANCE

ISBN:978-0-9975757-7-4

http://www.maichelev.com

Set List

DELIVERANCE

And I don't know a soul who's not been battered
I don't have a friend who feels at ease
I don't know a dream that's not been shattered
Or driven to its knees

            — Paul Simon, "American Song"

Dedication

This collection is dedicated to the brave and enlightened American son, Chris Hedges. Endgame politics are never unanimous! Listening to his speeches the last few years has helped me to become a more serious person.

You would not think to look at him, but he was famous long ago…

Out

Ok…

News…

Unexpected homelessness

Pandemic economics

All activity forward centers around the car

And Everything that Goes with it

Nobody wants to know much about what they do
Or what they've done
Instead, everybody wants to be Carly Simon
Or Sean Connery
Circa '66 to '71
Hey Jive
Can you dig it?
You can have it all
And everything that goes with it

Nobody wants to know what they do
Or what they've done
I've seen your dark side, Mister
I've got your number
And its equation
Its product
Its sum
Its quotient
You can have it all
And everything that goes with it

I live above a dirty bookstore
No, not the one on Meridian
The one off of Main
I clean up after my roommates
Linda, Gale, and Vivian

A labor of love
Shame; it's a shame
I live the life I love
And I love the life I live
And if you believe that
For fifty cents I'll tell you another one
And you can have it all
And everything that goes with it

Nobody wants to know much
About what they do or what they've done
How much did you spend
To make your car look like leprosy's contagion?
Junior's daycare this year
Was the money you spent on it
And you can have it all
And everything that goes with it

Junior ended up in a penitentiary
A danger to society
Classical symptoms of an industrial disease
A monetary squeeze
Serious menace
Next patient, please[1]
Ding!
Customized it
A strange corvette

---

1   Mark Knopfler, "Industrial Disease"

You can have it all
And everything that goes with it

Join the choir
Sing the chorus
Take your place on the pulpit
The harder they fall
The deeper they fall in it
Pull yourself together...
It was a Continental limo
Filled with rummage sale swap shop shit
Don't get upset
Skipping off the front steps
Didn't we almost have it all
And everything that goes with it

Zika Virus Tuesday

That was truly painful today
That slum with open sewers
Where the mosquito eggs were laid
Zika documentary
National Geographic story

Hurt so bad for those babies
Hurt so bad for the moms
No one is prepared for that
Could be you
Could be me
No one alive could have a heart that loving
That strong
Makes you want to collapse
No one's prepared for that

It was truly painful today
Thought to change the channel
But look at that…
May God have mercy!

Lithium, Seroquel, Gabapentin

One issue of depression
Its unarrested continuance
A concept
A condition
A diagnosis
A disease

Depression
A word so widely used
It has been rendered impotent and archaic
Humdrum
Banal
Who mentions its thievery?
Where once you'd easily identify with something
    insignificant
With a little laugh
Or by something touching
Moved to tears
Depressive measure can plow someone under in its
    troubling grasp
Rumination
Its pull
To be downcast
Then a parent dies
Or an old friend
And life becomes nothing but cruel

Dark and meaningless

Unfair

Depressives don't roll with any spiritual hopefulness

Any grace from dreams

Any optimism

They're *depressed*

They don't pick up

A palsied instrument with broken strings

The day's paradiddles and spring-loaded riffs

Aren't gathered with any wholesome personal talent

You cannot characterize the depressed as "loving"

The defeat and weight of depression sets in

Anger

Cynicism

Coldness

Abuse

Sadness

Depression

Long-term depression is a thing of the soul

It's not enough to say they don't have enough to do

No…

There's something going on in there

Recreational drugs

Self-medicating

A rocking Texas road house

Is a lot more exciting than adhering to the requirements

Of new homeopathic trends in antidepressive therapy

Be honest with the psychiatrist…

Completely honest

To be set straight

To find some discipline for discipline's sake

To walk across Alabama

Or a mile for a Camel

Kawasaki lets the good times roll

Selective Memory: A Talmudic Truth

Selective memory…
The inevitable

Speak of subjects…
Almost never of people

Off-Handed

Things we do off-handed
Things that fall in our laps
So much we never intend to do

I met the woman Mick Jagger dated
After he and Bianca split
She rented me a room in Coconut Grove
She brought the three tenors together
Pavarotti
Domingo
Carreras

I looked at a small, framed photograph
On her table of memories and asked
"Is that a picture of Margo Hemingway?"
"Yes," she said
"Margo and I were friends"

If I never knew what it was to feel my own voice singing...

All the King's Men
(Performed by Jude Law)

The friend of your youth is the only friend you will ever have, for he does not really see you. He sees in his mind a face that does not exist anymore, speaks a name — Spike, Bud, Skip, Red, Rusty, Jack, Dave — which belongs to that now nonexistent face. He's still the young idealist you used to be. He still sees good and bad in black and white. And men are sinners or saints ... but never both.

Well... This is Me

Do you hear voices?
Voices?
No, it's not auditory
It's neural
And it's rare
It's subtle connection
Neither terrifying nor disturbing
But from a higher reasoning
Beyond your own

To tell people you hear voices
Does not inspire confidence
It's nothing too very scientific
To a believer
No explanation is necessary
For a non-believer
No explanation will do

A Beautiful Day in the Neighborhood

The Jazz DJ up here
Is like one of those boy scouts just out of voice school
Worried most about whether his ounce of hipness
Isn't too Ted Baxter

I noticed the other day while folding my clothes
That there's a generation of Limbaugh linguists at
   the microphone
The acolytes know or don't know
They have the fat man's disease
His subcortextural growl
His pausal *humpff*
His regurgitative garble

And just as creepy…
The dude who took over Prairie Home Companion
Seems unable to do anything but emulate Garrison
Syllable-for-syllable
Accent on a leash
Two hours running
You noticed?
Garrison lives in us all
In some very legitimate way
But it's over
Did you know you can order Powdermilk Biscuits for
   next-day delivery?

Are you getting enough ketchup?
Prove yourself, mandolin man
Give us something original
You can't imitate and expect enthusiasm and loyalty
Regroup or go away
Deep breath now
Am I just being a hard-ass today?

I miss the 8:30 am Poetry Corner
Garrison was more than okay in every way
So what if he went for a little nookie?
That was his greater conflict, anyhow

NPR's politics changes lanes like a drunk on the highway

Lionized[2]

Well, the rifleman's stalking the sick and the lame
Preacherman seeks the same
Who'll get there first is uncertain
Nightsticks and water cannons
Tear gas
Padlocks
Molotov cocktails
And rocks behind every curtain

False-hearted judges
Dying in the webs that they spin
Only a matter of time 'til night comes steppin' in

Jokerman, dance...

---

2   Bob Dylan, *Infidels.* "Jokerman." Columbia records, 1983

Thurgood Marshall

Thurgood Marshall
Now there's a name
Thurgood Marshall
Once in a while he'd look up on his understudy
His assistant
And say
"Git 'er done, negro"
And they'd both look up and smile

Black folk got love 'cause they got each other
Which is more than us
Denzel Washington
There's a name
And Thurgood Marshall
Tall and firm as a mountain is high and wide

What Do You Know?

What do *you* know?
Thirty years I been workin'
Thirty!
Getting up t' do what has to be done
That's what I been doin'!
How I been livin'!
See these tired eyes
Looks like an eagle blinking!
I know you're sleepin' late in your bed, Dave
What do you know from heavy liftin'?
Bitch!

What do you know?
What do you know about sittin' in traffic?
It's like having a flat soda habit
Traffic is like being an Elmer's glue addict
Yes, it's like being in chains
Being in chains is every bit as tragic
Traffic!
Don't let it sap your spirit
Traffic
FM
Sing it!
Traffic
America…

You're not dreamin' it
Traffic

> *Damn this traffic jam*
> *How I hate to be late*
> *It hurts my motor to go so slow*
> *Damn this traffic jam*
> *Time I get home my supper 'll be cold*
> *Damn this traffic jam*[3]

What do *you* know?
No one *ever* gets a raise
No one *ever* has a dime
The cost of living goes up and up
Time after time after time
And kids...
All they do is ask for money
I've got no maid
Girlfriend likes to go out on the town and wine and dine
I don't mean to be so down on it all...
All the time
What do *you* know?
Hard work
Hard work is the whole nine yards
That's a steel dump truck full of sand
He don't wear gloves

---

3   Taylor, James. "Damn this Traffic Jam." *JT.* Colombia/Sony Legacy. 1977

His is like paws

Two calloused hands

An eighteen-wheeler stacked with boxes

Too heavy to lift

Too big to get ahold of

Behind those doors

Behind those locks…

You're not exactly overjoyed to have this job

It's a big payload and the driver keeps checkin' his watch

Warehouse dust

Ramp

Sweat

Lunch truck

Cooler

Steel toe

Weight belt

Piss in this jar

Workingman's Dead

He sleeps like a baby

Nativity scene in the yard

As Simple as This

It took me twenty-five years to write
Something as simple as this

Must 've Been

Must've been a wheat field on your tongue

Waving

Or two-dozen blueberry muffins

Fresh out of the oven

With powdered sugar topping

Craving!

You must have once dated a troubled Vincent van Gogh

Or turned the head of a twenty-year old Michelangelo

You must've played Bingo in Ft. Knox, Tennessee

You must've hitched a ride in the hills of Modena, Italy

Must've come down with the chickenpox

Or mononucleosis

Or lupus

Or Godforbid, all three

Must've sat too close to the citronella wax

You must have lost your wallet in New York City

Y' must've been the first person to t' rub two sticks together

You must've chased a bear out of a cave

Couldn't stand the weather

Aila...

Must've been the date of expiration

On the peas and carrots in the cupboard

Must've been a few too many Novembers

I know Mr. Bill sleeps in your medicine cabinet

Must be that Mr. Bubble knows how to fix your bath
Just the way you like it
Must've been that the sorority was on double-secret probation
Must've been the club bitch of a biker gang
That never stops crossing the nation

Must've learned the English language
From the Saturday matinee
Must've been that your grasp exceeded your reach
Having put all your faith in a figure of speech
Must've done something
That down in your soul was an act of treason

Must 've been the caramelized onion
Next to the jalapeño lid
She bought a second-hand flute
And chased all the rats in Manhattan into the Hudson,
    she did

Must 've been "Silver Bells…"
Silver bells
Silver bells
It's Christmas time in the city
Ring-a-ling
Jing-a-ling
Soon it will be Christmas Day

Tours on Tours, Dread on Dread

I pray I never live in a society that practices scarification

That is not to speak of male circumcision

Which is an act of cleanliness

Tatooing...?

Ask Hobbes

Big Chick Singer

We've got a big chick singer
She's a primed twenty-eight
Huge voice
Pretty face
Killer ass
Boss rack
A star in the making if I've ever seen one
Polished
She can pull it off with just bass, guitar, and drums
I swear to you…
She's Nancy Wilson
If she's not all of Pat Benetar
The teens 'll *eat her up*
The twenty-somethings 'll grab the album, too
We've got the makings of a big rock 'n' roll show here

Who did Sheryl Crow's production?
Now…
The songs…
Nothing cheesy…
Likeable…
Hard-edged…
Think Joan Jett, 1981
Mixed with Avril and that chick from Concrete Blonde
This girl is *money!*

Gotta get some pretty boys up there

No hippies

A touch of glam

A little gothic

Kinda heroin chic

A pent-up Duran Duran

Wake 'em up to eat and jam

Yeah…

A girl…

They're always the best

Put 'em on stage

Have 'em undress[4]

Maybe a pianist who's a trained accompanist

No one on stage beyond their thirtieth

Gotta be a young wreckin' crew

Call your man at Berkeley

Duets are big now

Why don't we find some hungry poet son-of-a-bitch who can
remember his lines?

She can declare war on him until intermission

Then he can state his case

Stand his ground

We'll post his broken dreams up on fifty-foot screens

I can see it now!

---

4   Tom Petty, "The Last DJ"

An encore of redemption
Love, hope, and unity
Now *that's* what I call music…
If y' give 'em two tour busses
They'll ask for three
New York
London
Paris
Munich

Ain't I Mr. Kincade from the Partridge Family?
This is how it was back in the day
A sexy, singin' piece of ass is still a money tree

"What's her name, boss?"

"Like I'd tell *you*…
You snatched Rita from me!"

Bobby Peru

Waddya think of that coke?

Didn't even taste like an old stick of gum in the junk drawer
Just hard on the body
There are people who get shot on street corners
For peddling this bootleg shit
I give my American dollar bills
For this bogus, perfumed garbage from a meth factory
Off the Jersey Turnpike somewhere
I did everything but throw it away

Fuck!
Bobby, you told me you had connections…

Well Maiche, I do
But y' got to rob a bank to get a pouch…

My Sorry *Zafftieg*

In the next life

If I'm so blessed…

I'm sure I'll be raised in the house between the moyle's and
    the scribe's

Deborah Winger will live down the street

She'll be my big sister's best friend

I'll show off whenever I'm near her

And she'll think I'm cute

And I'll speak her name

Each night after I say my prayers and go to sleep

Rushmore

Listenin' to Neil Young
Is to find y' heels again
And it rained all day
And the sunset was peach

Father...

You can't afford 375,000 dollars
To sit on a couch in New York City for ten years
Pussyfootin' around with Dr. Whoeverkowitz
But you can confess your hang-ups to a priest
Or talk to a rabbi
Straight up...
They're not only about salvation or damnation
They know Freud and Jung and Fromm
If they're worth their weight in salt

To divulge and confess is preferable to curmudgeonhood
Get things off your chest
Or your heart will be caged and die
Father, of this I'm bothered...
Help me see through this morass

Father...
I did some things when I was younger
I can't swallow, now
And ... and I'm not the man I'd like to be
I took a wrong turn and just kept going

Father...

Falconry School

Retentive ebullience
Every day an extra mile…
Come on in the water's great

The Greatest

The greatest generation

The greatest nation

The greatest cities

The greatest form of government

The greatest military

The land of opportunity

The greatest show on earth

Education

"Politicians have traditionally hidden behind three things:
   the flag, the bible and children.

No child left behind
No child left behind!
Oh really…?
It wasn't long ago you were talking about giving children a
   head start!
Head start?
Left behind?

Someone's losing fucking ground here."

— George Carlin

Forgive Some Trespass

Forgive some trespass
For you do not realize all of your own

Song with Accordion

The other night I got into bed
And I guess it really got to me that I was alone
I became upset
I shook with emotion
Like the wind had been knocked out of me
I caught my breath …
But I couldn't…
It was like years of anguish had me shuddering

The cocaine I'd done the day before
Must have squared me up some, I imagine
That's the way it is sometimes
Delayed emotion
Vulnerability

My Son's Girlfriend

My son's girlfriend is twenty-three or twenty-four like him
She calls herself "Becca"
Couldn't quite fit into *"Re*-becca"
A beautiful, biblical name
She's chestnut
Clear-voiced

Women are to my son like a cat is to a child...
A young child
Something to follow and play with
These generations...
He's got enough conversation skills to get himself scratched
   up pretty good
Love and laughter
Teasin'
Pleasin'

Becca...
Who I've been in the same room with once at a family dinner
Has a face that comes together in an athletic strength
   and cuteness
Her nose kind of rolls on the lowline
Giving her a gentile's strewn way
You might think she was an all-American skier
On a white mountain
In a colorful knit hat

With an Olympic smile
You might think she was a furry forest creature
You might surmise she was once a brave English knight
I am not flattering my son's girlfriend
I am merely describing her
Becca
Levi and Becca

If he chooses her to be amongst the forty percent of people
   who stay married
And if she chooses him to trust and count on and open up to
   and love
I say they will have chosen wisely
You can sense good chemistry
If she's the ladder up
He's the bridge across
Winds within winds
Their waters run deep
Sunshine above
What fathers see that sons don't know…

The lessons of life can't be learned in a day
He hungers for what is *his* idea of good times
High times…
Real times

She'd really like to give him everything
But her game plan isn't thirty goin' on forty

Doing nothing
Thinking about camping out at some music festival
What passes by that we'd dive for later?
They're *all* the one that got away, dear boy

You meet a few people in your life
Who help you begin
Over and over again

Imagine her trying to gain his heart
Imagine him uncannily wanting it to be brought to an end
Freedom…

Freedom is just letting enough time to go by to allow the
    feeling of waste to set in

A young father and mother on their way
Such a good thing to see
Twenty-three like her
Twenty-four like him
Levi and Becca

The Song You Haven't Written

There's always the song you haven't written
Like finding twenty dollars in the pocket of your jeans
Like déjà vu
Or the flash of some long-forgotten dream
Like the worm at the bottom of your tequila bottle
Like something all your own
That five minutes before had no title
Like a cat walking slow with something colorful in its mouth
Like a chemist stumbling onto penicillin
Like getting into the bath with dirty feet
Like walls tumbling down…
Finally…

The song you haven't written
Like tripping over your shoelaces
A jigsaw puzzle's last few pieces
A five-finger discount
A butcher's knife in a soapy sink
A Hail Mary pass on the very last play
Like a pelican breaking to dive

I am the eagle
I live in high country
In rocky cathedrals
That reach to the sky

I am the hawk
There's blood on my feathers
The time is still turning
They soon will be dry [5]

Singer-songwriters

Like only Joe Strummer did it so rude
Like a blacked-out city

Don't ask me nothin' 'bout nothin'
Cuz I just might tell ya the truth [6]

The song you haven't written
Like wine spilt on a tablecloth
Like a moth to a flame
A flame to a moth…
Like your first whiff of Sweetgrass braid
Like walkin' out of Charlie's with a good six-string, paid

Inspiration…
Move me brightly [7]

5   Denver, John. "The Hawk and the Eagle"
6   Dylan, Bob. "Outlaw Blues"
7   Garcia, Jerry. "Terrapin Station"

Simple Words

Follow your interests

Three simple words
If only to recognize first
What interests you most
College kids wonder
If they can see themselves as a doctor or a lawyer
An engineer or a broker
What does business school teach?

Opportunities are limited for marine biologists
But then again…
The times have changed
You don't make much as a teacher
But what could be greater than turning kids on every day?

I've known a few paramedics
Who will tell you, "It's a war out there"
A cop walks out of his house
With a gun on his belt every day
The American landscape…
Some simple advice from another somnambulist citizen
Follow your interests
What else?

The Time and the Place

Honesty is the best policy
The truth is always there to rely on
To carry you over
Pull you through

When it is that some truths hit too hard
Where figurative honesty requires more than you can muster
And the honest move
Is a cane to the head…

Someday Never Comes

People come here and lose sight of their innocence
They fall in with people who likewise have lost good sense
New Orleans is bigger than death and smaller than life
Look at that one
You can tell he's really into his Buck knife
And this one here keeps saying everything to me twice

Who are you punishing?
What are you so angry at?
Where do you go to clear your head?
Is this how it all spirals out of control?
You didn't give yourself a chance
A chance to take a bite out of the life
That lay just ahead

He'll call you a bitch and tell you to shut up
Waiting for the shit to come
Spent corners of the French Quarter…
It ain't a glass of rosé in the late afternoon

Ooh look, girl
Let me take a look at you
Biscuit
Croissant
Baguette

Crêpe suzette
Bon bons, Wolfie
Dilly Beans, Marci
Pralines
Chocolat Fondue

You're invited, but your friend can't come

Dress her up
Give her the good stuff
You know the drill, Phil
Put her on the dance floor
See to it she meets El Señor
Keep the driver on call past dawn
Phil, she's cherry
Keep an eye on her
So young

Innocence
What's the opposite?
Experience
The screaming hallucinogenic barcode
Of multi-orgasmic sadomasochistic potluck genetics
Come share a bench with a local who don't share benches
Here, like anywhere, the inopportune become opportunistic
This is the restaurant at the end of the universe
The special tonight is lamb — skewered on stick

Evangeline!
Evangeline!
My oh my, the years have been kind
The sad overdose's dealer has the busiest line
I love this place
5000 houses of rotting wood
The best of my generation
They got away with what they could

Yes, I like this place
Sunshine on your face
Fog off the river
Cloak and dagger
Drunk
Really drunk
Hey Stagger...
Is that you, Stagger?

Baby, you were Vassar
You were Smith, Radcliffe, Bryn Mawr
Your own house
Your own man
A big dog
My God ... children!
Nice clothes
A new car
You look like a street urchin from Seattle

You see through all this hokey voodoo
But your veins are filled with Fiddlefaddle

Children
To protect
To mentor
To parent and love
She has his eyes and your spirit
What are you doin' here in those swanky lace gloves?

You'll learn what vice brings
But you won't learn it too soon
Someday never comes
Leave a note…
Or don't
Someday never comes, child
Someday never comes…

You meet some folks out in America
You meet some folks in the city of New Orleans
The youth hunt in packs
They do
And the whole time you're there
There's something in the air
That's twice as needy
Twice as seedy
And Lord, Lord…
Twice as shrewd

Don Lemon

Don Lemon is God suffering

He wants and needs

To morph into someone or something else

Every day he takes to the CNN news desk

And quickly demonstrates

That something poisonous

Has just bitten him

A Hundred Men

A hundred men
Their … enthusiasms
Their … ideologies
And no one gets hurt…

A few *live* for the Milwaukee Bucks
A few have season tickets
A few work for the government as forest rangers
None are better than James Comey
A few are born with defective organs
A few have difficult birthmarks
A few get cirrhosis of the liver

Some try to learn the guitar at some point
One becomes a priest of some religion
Six are lawyers (at least that many)
Some have the sexual affects of country veterinarians
Some hold a potential for greater violence
All need to borrow money at some point
Some still seethe using the word "nigger"

When the confederate statues started to be removed
Over the last few years in Jacksonville and Pensacola
And Mobile and down to New Orleans
Flags were being changed

And coming down
And the names of the high schools and such…
Lee Circle
Jackson Junior High…
Well, there was a dude in his pick-up truck
With a big confederate flag mounted in back
Trying his damnedest to peel out at the intersections
    around town
Does a guy like that accelerate into a crowd?
Someone does
One of 'em
(Rest in peace, Heather Heyer)

One-hundred men
One of 'em's in jail
One of 'em's in a trailer park
(Every trailer park got a pharmacy and a Sugar Shack and a
    hock shop)

I want to go to Detroit
And walk around in a hoodie for a year
I want to go to Camden, New Jersey
And be PTA president

I want to fly above the fracked Appalachians in a helicopter
With Chris Hedges and Joe Sacco eating veggie burgers
And slammin' enough Glenlivet

To properly vomit like dragons above it all
That'll set you back a few hundred-grand!

Buy my books!
I'll tell you how it goes, man

Says Here: Part 3

I was only taking orders

Evil

Newfound glory via firing squads

Evil

Premeditated gang rape

Evil

Alcohol poisoning, hazing

Evil

Preemptive action in the intelligence world

Evil

Superstition

Evil

Population control

Evil

"You don't have to do this"

Evil

61-inch television sets and a free bowl of soup

Evil

Unionbusters

Evil

Three-eyed conspiratorial shock jocks

Evil

Cheap, affordable, devitalized foods

Evil

The space program as something admirable

Evil

Seven deadly sins

Evil

When the fun begins

Evil

Undiagnosed bi-polar suckiness

Evil

Increasing your worth at someone else's expense

Evil

Ethnic cleansing

Evil

Rednecks showing off for one another

Evil

An evil past in an evil world

Evil

Evil rockstardom

Evil wannabees

Evil executives

The executioner's face is always well hidden

Evil

The most reviled disciple has no saint

Evil

I don't care how big you say you are

History is just going to roll right over you

Evil

He who dies with the most toys wins!

Evil

Loopholes a plenty

Evil

The hoax of free speech

Evil

Look deep into my eyes…

Evil

Water table spoilage

Evil

Vladimir Putin's grip on power

Evil

This inadequacy in the White House

Steering the outcome of an American election

Evil

Holy water for eleven dollars a pop on TV

Evil

Steven King's bloody prurience

Evil

(Why subject yourself to it?)

Misery is the river of the world

Evil

400 years of slavery

Evil

What a man won't do to own a Lamborghini

Evil

Twenty bucks and a bus ticket home

Evil

Evil can manifest itself in you or me

Evil

Evil wants to take you on a "what only gets worse" tour

Really
Evil

Sinner's Prayer

The sinner's prayer
Only one y' seem t' hear
There's always someone wounded
Or threatening to get there

The sinner's prayer
Everybody's got a story to tell
I've heard of 'em but I've never seen an angel
The sinner don't pray a prayer
He just goes with what's there to go with
Heaven sent
People don't do what they believe in
They just do what's most convenient
And then they repent[8]

Sinner's prayer
It's a free country
I'm not hurting anyone
Everybody's doin' it
And I feel so light and free when I'm done

Sinner's prayer
Nobody ever sinned in New York City
San Francisco or New Orleans

---

8   Bob Dylan, *Kocked Out Loaded,* "Brownseville Girl."
Columbia Records, 1986

Unless it turns black and falls off…
They don't know what sin even means
Have I sinned against you?
Have you done the same?
What it is to wear clothes so dirty
What it is to keep your hands clean

Sin…
To settle on a compromised version of yourself
Life must sometimes get lonely
The ABCs of the diseases of mental health
His favorite song was "Leader of the Pack"
Hers: "You Don't Own Me"

Sinner's prayer
Sin is sin because sin begets sin
I've already confessed
Don't need to confess again
Sin is sin because sin begets sin
You play things the way you play things
Who you were at the time…
Sin is sin because sins begets sin
First we know nothing
Then we know less…

This little light of mine…
This little light of mine…

What Do You Do? (Uncle David)

What do you do
When for all good reason you're feeling sorry for yourself?
Oh, brother…
What do y' do
When your body language *is* like a version of someone else?
I is another…

What do y' do
When you've broken up your things again?
Stare at the wall…

What do y' do
When your bird that whistles has lost the song he sings?
Cocaine and alcohol

What do y' do
When you walk the floor
And wonder why with every breath you breathe?[9]
God!

And you ain't got anywhere to go
'Cept that place where you end up on your knees?
Cat Stevens
Harold and Maude

---

9 Bob Dylan, *The Times, They Are a Changin',* "The Ballad of Hollis Bown"
Columbia Records, 1964

What do y' do
When there's no home sweet home?
All those empty habits

What y' do
When the mirror shows a sad old man?
Who's that?
That's…

What do y' do
When the events of your life don't turn out the way
   y' planned?
Don't look back

Who never really took a stand?
Who never buckled down?
Who took the easy way out?
The village idiot's in town
Man … oh, man…
Who knew but never did?
Who lost interest in *everything?*
Who got soft?
Who hid?
Who surrendered?
Who lost the ring?

Don't ya just hate the holidays?

Here's the phone

It's uncle David

Oh Yeah! Daylight Savings Time

Oh yeah

Surprise yourself

Oh yeah

A bill of good health

Oh yeah

Strike while the iron's hot

You sure knocked 'em dead, sweetheart

Oh yeah

Whatever works for you

Oh yeah

Y' gotta do what y' gotta do

Oh yeah

You are right from your side and I am right from mine

You win

I win

We lose

Every time

The sky is falling

Oh yeah

Passion is for maniacs and teenagers, darlin'

Oh yeah

Went back to New York City

None of the stores were where they were before

Oh yeah

Here's the bank with the digital deficit counter!

Chock Full o' Nuts was all outta that smooth creamer
Gave a guy twenty bucks
He said, "I'll be back; you wait here"
Oh yeah
I fancy a pint
Let's go suffer at the open mic
Oh yeah
Washington, DC when the cherry blossoms are in bloom
If you believe … they put a man on the moon
Oh yeah
I've got a job
My job is to mope
It wouldn't be so bad if things got any better
To mope
Get better it don't
Oh yeah
Happy anniversary, honey!

A Black Woman

You've got a career that puts a fine suit on your back
And good standing out in the suburbs
Strolling through the Santa Monica Ritz-Carlton at the
    Evinrude Trim Tabs Convention
You see Iman's royal niece moving by in steps

A black woman is an *event*
Copper love
Resident soul
And right *there*

Dark queen
Lady Dread

May I hold the door?

TENNIS SHOES.

THE "PETTITT" MATCH SHOE.

This is our *latest* in tennis shoes, and is used in preference to all other kinds by the Court Tennis Champion, Mr. Thos. Pettitt, after whom the shoe is named, and numerous other players of note.

Style No. 6. Is made of fine brown canvas, trimmed with French calf, hand sewed, and soled with our celebrated heavy, pure red rubber "Match Sole," with smooth bottom, which is equally well adapted for grass, dirt, cinder, or board courts. None genuine without our name stamped on each sole, and " Pettitt " inside . . . . price, per pair, $5.50

Style No. 7.   Same as No. 6, only made of fine drab English buckskin „ „ „ 8.00
Style No. 8.   Same as No. 6, only made of white buckskin . . „ „ „ 8.00
Style No. 8½. Same as No 8, only high laced . . . . „ „ „ 9.50
Style No. 9.   Same as No. 6, only made of French calfskin . . „ „ „ 6.50
Style No. 9½. Same as No. 9, only high laced . . . . „ „ „ 7.50

Nos. 11 and 12.

No. 10.

Nos. 13 and 11.

No. 14.

TENNIS SHOES.

No. 10.   New spiked sole tennis shoe, French calf, hand sewed $2.50
No. 11.   Extra quality French calf, hand sewed, corrugated red rubber sole . . 5.00
No. 11½. Russet leather, high laced, pyramid sole 4.50
No. 12.   Good quality, russet leather, pyramid sole. An excellent shoe for the price . 3.00
No. 14.   Fine canvas, corrugated soles 1.50

17

Tennis Anyone?
(One-Hundred Names)

Tennis courts in little white shorts

Toy cup Pomeranians and ruffles under short white skirts

Wrong!

Tennis is fierce

Firing

Fast

Jimmy Connors' backhand off a Wilson A2000 was a
cannon blast!

The sport of tennis was born out of the age of the duel

Medieval society's awful vestige

Honor pure

Ever cruel

Before the gun

Sheffield steel

Wilkinson

You have offended my sense of honor!

En garde you scoundrel!

You killed my father; prepare to die!

You look at my wife?

To the dueling tree!

You imp!

You wretch!

And then one or both men died

(Campy, wouldn't you say?)

Tennis anyone?

From the sword

A racquet

Simple as that

English etiquette

A ball

A court with a net

A sport was born

Late 16th century news

What their tennis shoes must have looked like!

Ruddy cheeks

Sweat

Tournament

Game

Point

Match

Set

350 years later a stadium watches

Vijay Armritraj and Adriano Panatta

Battle in Conway, New Hampshire

The Volvo classic

The summer of '79

The roster

The scoreboard

The draft

Rankings

We've got tickets!

I think Pam Shriver was there with back problems

Tracy Austin was sixteen years old

Chris Evert with her Jack Kramer wooden stick

Talk about a class act…!

Chrissie, a blonde, beautiful lioness

With a handful of championships

Wilson and Dunlop and Bancroft sold a lot of wood
    tennis racquets

AMF and Prince stepped in with metal and graphite

And found the sweet spot with the oversized models

Clay court

Hard court

Wimbledon grass

Catgut strings

Nylon

Synthetic

Different tensions

Different gauges

Different strokes

Different grips

Different games

North Shore Park *belonged* to James Schor

And Harry Pliskin and Andy Krantz and Ross Dubbins

And Ilene and Faye and Jackie P

And Lois Abrams and Amy Perkel and Robin Leoni …
    the divine

And Gayle Golden

Eileen Kaufman practiced down the block at Polo Park with
her white-bearded father
She was a few years older than me
I'd sit in the roots of an old banyan tree and watch them hit
Fierce!
I knew I'd never be that good
That *on*
That consistent
How to expend that level of energy
And always an inch over the net
That banyan is still there
Though the courts have become a baseball diamond
I never did introduce myself
Her daddy was unsmiling

I began taking lessons on those public courts
I wore through many a pair of Nikes in the South Florida sun
Deeply tanned
I was ranked top-150 in the state of Florida at some point in
my teens
I had a good twisting serve and I used a western grip
Like the great Swede, Bjørn Borg we watched
I loved the slide of clay over the punishing hard courts
I never took it much further than that great enjoyment I felt
as a kid
Which is a shame 'cause it was something I did well
And it'd probably deliver me from all this endless
cigarette action

We'd play for hours and go to McDonalds

And come back all Whoppered up

To slug it out all afternoon

North Shore and Flamingo Park

Our tennis Meccas

I'd lose my temper from time to time

I picked up a few trophies

I got *wiped* by Aaron Krickstein

At the Junior Orange Bowl classic one year

Jim Courier and all the Bolleteri boys and girls were *assassins*

Francisco Montana came into the world with tennis balls
   in his crib

He used to whoop ass on Andre Agassi at 12 and 14

Being on the court with these proteges was to be flat
   outclassed

To be made a toddler again

Aaron Krickstein at thirteen years of age was just
   downright skilled

He did me in under 35 minutes

Including warm-ups

He used a red pro AMF racket

He walked on the court with a *stack* of 'em

It's fierce!

Fast!

Intense!

Savage!

Go to a professional match some day
You won't be bored
Put it on your early bucket list
These pros have the control and talent
To unleash all their strength
Unlike anything you've seen before
It's unreal
A battle
It is *ferocity* on a court!
You hardly know there's big money in the air
Pride
World-ranking
Recognition
Notoriety
Sponsorship
A tennis tournament is another world

I haven't picked up a racquet with any regularity for
    forty years
And I'm not the better for it
I played well
And on those few times that I have played since
The experience filled me with joy
For its eye-hand coordination
Its footwork
Its strokes so round and exaggerated…
Great fun
Tennis anyone?

Alyssa Lipshultz learned under her father's tutelage

Mr. Dave Lipshultz

Who bore cannons at Flamingo Park

Dave would have his beginners hold the racquet down with

    two hands

Like an aluminum fishing net

He had them Miaggi like that for a year or more

Like they were scooping up a trout

Until he'd let them loose

And they'd start hitting naturally with a powerful stroke

Miagi

Dave Lipshultz knew how to build a player

Alan Zabelinsky had a beautiful left-handed game

The Shapiro brothers flourished on the court

    with Lipshultz

His sons played

I'd love to see them again

All of them observant, orthodox Jews

My father, Doctor Morton Weinstein

He played after seeing patients till 3:00 or 4:00

My dad grew up playing tennis in Richmond, Virginia

On the same public courts where Arthur Ashe would

    later play

They called him "Doc" or "Morty"

And he had a serve that came with a *roar*

In his eighties now

He still loves a clay court in the sun

Let's see…

There were some characters down there at Flamingo

There was Sy the cabby

Skinny with a cigar in the afternoon

What a voice

And a gritty way about him

There was a Rastafarian who'd light up a spliff every day
on court

A blonde man who wore Converse All-star leather high-tops

He loved the scriptures

Always talking Jesus

Havi Holtz was a wonder boy

So handsome, blue-eyed, and pretty

You tended to watch him somehow

Mitchell Cogan's kinky, curly hair

A little chubby with some *latkes* in tin foil

He used Yonex racquets

Different and cutting-edge at the time

Me and Joey Edelstein played a lot

J.J. and Danny Simonson were competitive to a fault

Jimmy Feinberg up north with a great love for the game

Max Cohen's whole family played

All of these people worked and found time in the late afternoon to squeeze in a few sets

We've got three; need a fourth

Every kind of face

It was good to be there with Sandy Biegelman

And Adam and Gayle Golden

Larry Kutun and David Stoneberg and Peter Russin and
   Carrie Meyers and lil' Jen

Jay Burger and Rob Lewis

The Zarons, Eric Prosnitz, and David Schnur

And Scotty Davis and Sarah Stein

David Williams and the Farnsworths

Shaheed and Cheffica Mucadam

Elliot Grub and his pop

David Berkowitz

We lost him one summer

A king upon the earth

Cindy Phillips and her Israeli mother

And Pammy Blue Eyes

Dr. Korn

Dr. Russin

Perry Fabian

Gerry Stein and me—little David Weinstein

I shall buy a racquet and a can of balls

And I will find a wall to hit against

Tennis anyone?

Modern Cinema

What do I know?
Making movies via formula
With stencil
And brace
For *watchability*
So boring at length
The overcompensation of violence
Must be *bigger*
Faster
Sexier
KABOOM!
Hollywood caught on to it in all of one day
And so it was
And so it is

Subtitles in our little theater still makes it, though
I've got the blanket...
You ready, honey?

Old New Orleans Preacher, Sunday AM Radio

Lying in bed one chilly morning
At Marquette House on Carondelet
In a too-spacious brick room
Built a century-and-a-half ago
Its windows wide from floor to ceiling
I tampered with the frayed wires of a clock-radio
And heard an old New Orleans Preacher
Rasp through the static on the dial:
Love is more than a feelgood emotion

He addressed his congregation
Love is more than a feelgood emotion

He admonished the younger generation
Love is more than a feelgood emotion

Years later, I still hear that voice
Beseeching his flock with caring and concerned authority

Love is more than a feelgood emotion

Old New Orleans preacher
Sunday AM radio

Standing There

To find a less attractive one
To know her golden heart
That's God's work
She thought she'd never know love
Thought she was untouchable
Lesser

'Cause of you
Now she's locked in rapture
Go find her
She will carry your seed to greater glory
Homely
The diva's only wild
Practically spastic
And the trophy wife
She's trippin' the same … all the time

So…
If you wanna be happy for the rest of your life…

Takamine Sunburst

Gabriella…

When you dropped me off on 79th Street

After song night at the Luna Star

As I closed the door

I caught sight of your boyish, dark-eyed Italian face

And I knew I could take you to me

For a long time

Gabriella

Michener's Cane

Funny…
I've never thought of you as a being with girl parts, Jo…
Though recently you've appeared in dreams
Naked as a jaybird in dress socks and Capezios
There was a silver pole through the hardwood floor in my
    living room
You were being chased and poked by a man with his hand on
    his own hardware
Handsome devil
The two of you seemed to be enjoying your little exhibition
I woke thinking of something
But I don't remember what it was…
No, not at all
I broke something
I threw a chair
It was daytime

In my dreams your back is always to me
You look away with an expression pained
My bad feelings worsen
I don't know what you've become
The drunken marionette
Michener's cane

Discontent (Y' Been Robbed)

At some point during the last five-hundred years
A man held a pen and coined the phrase
"This be the season of my discontent"

Was he pointing his finger at others
As readily as he'd discovered his own frailty and swarth?

The season of my discontent...
We found out along the way that the monster who visits
Needs first his shoes mended

Come ... sit

Shoah (Holocaust)

Claude Lanzman's documentary, *Shoah* is haunting

Most cannot sit through it

A world at war is unfathomable in and of itself

Unless you've lived through one…

Survived one

The nine hours of *Shoah* is far-reaching

Into all that you've ever heard or read

About the inhumanity

The insane, diseased mind of Adolf Hitler — the accursed

The societies that fell in behind him

The apparatus of annihilation

Nothing in the film is sensationalized

Lanzman

A tall, heavyset man takes you to the forests

The train tracks

The formerly Jewish-owned houses and apartments

There's no music

Only interviews

From one or two camera angles

How the Hitler youth were desensitized

Survivors speaking

I watched it in Tell Aviv twenty-five years ago

Over two days

I'll watch it again

I've grown much too complacent

A Man Cannot…

A man cannot sit at a table with a father who touches
  his daughters

A man cannot sit at a table with a son who sleeps with
  his mother

A man cannot sit at a table with those revellers whose
  laughter comes to cackle

All Peoples

All peoples
Protect their own sacred way
Worn stone steps
Ancient cisterns
What we'd pin to the doorpost
To remind ourselves of
A hundred years in

So it Be

If one man took pause
To consider what the other had to swallow
Wouldn't it be a wonderful world?
What a wonderful world it would be

In some way we're all responsible
For one another's minds

Caring II

Caring hurts too much

Caring requires hope and selflessness

And a decency

Caring is vigilance

You keep vigilance or you drown in its consequences

And drowning is real

Caring

Patience

Caring

Sober-ness

Mom got a call and turned away for a second

For an instant

Caring

Trustworthiness

To be worthy of trust

If you felt everything there was to care about...

God, you'd evaporate into dust

Caring hurts too much

Give me emptiness from a box

Glorify vengeance

I don't care

Glamorize violence

And sex and sex and sex and sex and sex

I'll sit staring

Just put me to bed with a cleared conscience
Caring
My nurses' voices
Vee-vee, did you know you'd work like this when you chose
    healthcare in your career choices?
Caring
Yes, I feel deeply about these things you're sharing
Caring
I feel the turbulence in the depths of my conscience
Every time you offer deliverance
To the souls who's indulgence far outweighs their sustenance
Jesus!

Caring
Flamboyance
Caring
Annoyance
Caring
Those consequences...

He wasn't trying to be a hero
But hand him a halo
I just did it
Automatic
Caring

Some Mothers

Some mothers try to build a genius
Some mothers are always on the phone
Some mothers shoot intravenous
Some work their fingers to the bone

Some mothers spank their children
Two or three times a week
Some mothers hug their children
Cheek to cheek to cheek to cheek
Some mothers are so busy
They're never there
Some mothers sum things up
Tussling their little ones' hair

Some mothers have loving husbands
Much attuned to their spouse's heart
Some mothers are divorced
Before the good stuff even starts
Some mothers go to church
Bible study, too
Some mothers have to do
What they'd never choose to do

Some mothers join the Army
Y' seen 'em in their fatigues

Some mothers bring a crate of cold chocolate milk
To each game of little league

Some mothers lay in bed watching TV in bathrobes
With just enough Valium and Xanax to forget the dry-
  cleaning clothes
Some mothers have never missed a Miami Dolphins
  football game
Some mothers love the holidays
Some mothers are always in some kind of pain

Some mothers you remember better than others
From the old neighborhood
I've never sat back and tried to recall
I haven't … but I could

Joel's mom, Marcia
She called me "Honeyface"
Blue eyed
Red-headed
Loved to laugh
Good times on Lakeview place

Sean's mom, Carol
Olive skinned
Brown eyed
Engaging
She loved us

Lee's mom

Barbara

A New Yorker

A worrier

Once-divorced

Lee was kind o' spindly

Got bruised a lot

I'm sure she worried as my mother did

About another weekend playing football
   at Fischer Park

Ralph's mom was kind of the same way

Evette...

She wasn't sure about anyone but her family

And even they may not have made the mark

Lee Frank's mom was always skinny and a little bit older

She let Lee set up a full drum set in their living room

We didn't see much of her but she was around

Lee had a piano, too

Brenda Korn

Next door

Three kids

I remember her voice better than her face

Marble

Silver

Lladro

Whatever we thought of them
Whatever they thought of us

Bobby's mom…
She was like a shadow
Like a deer
Bobby had a lot of conflict with her
We piled in a car and went to see our buddy, Miles, in
    Georgia once
Bob got punished for like a year

The Stonebergs…
Sandy Stoneberg had three boys
And there was always a housefull of adolescents
Banging on the piano or raiding her fridge
She endured it all with a smile of resignation
She was all love
Huge smile with dimples!

And then there was Judy Kutun
Wife of legistlator, Bary Kutun
They lived near me on 47th Street
She was the loveliest of them all
I remember always trying to ask a better question
When she made Larry and me a sandwich
Larry always had amazing athletic ability
And Barry Kutun was a man's man

We must have given them what little kids give adults...
A lot of love and little worry

I'm sitting here writing
About the mothers I've never really thought about much
    since my youth
Jill's mom
My ex-mother in law
She was great
Never had a bad word for me
She loved a black man true
A piano-player named Alston
Two survivors
"Cacky" was her nickname
Loved Charles Aznavour!
Told me to, "Worry less about others and more about
    yourself"

What kind of mother is my ex-wife Jill?
I had so much respect for her
All I could do was behave and sit still
She's a hugger and a kisser
And you know that's always good to see
Her new husband has three girls
And Jill with three boys...
Yes, yes, the Bradys
Tim must be doing something right

She's like some exotic beauty
Her eyes wide-set
She's the picture of strength
The presence of grace
I see her at graduations every three or four years
I'm ok, but it does something to me
The way she moves
The way she steps
Her voice…

Some mothers have fourteen babies
Some women won't pick one up
Some mothers work in rice paddy fields
Baby drops out
Pick the baby up

Some mothers…
Some mothers…
Stacey's mom has got it goin' on!
Stacey's mom has got it goin' on!

Harold!

Harold!
That was your last date!

In Another Life

In another life
We'll probably be man and wife
Not the next life
Or the one after that
It'll take a while…
A long while
Before any of this comes to pass

Man and wife…
Children
I'll have them
I'll give them
We'll love
All this pain
Will have long been faded
We'll get caught in the rain
And kiss once again

Or one day we'll meet on the street
And for a moment there
We'll both be unable to speak
Hello…
It's you
And our eyes will reflect the helplessness
Oh God, there's something to this
Hello…

Have you ever seen yourself fall to your knees
And wrap your arms around somebody's waist
And you can't let go?

In another life
Maybe what's made manifest
Are the things you could never get past
Where all is new again…
In differences…
Our differences

In another life

Ancient Justice

If you put alcohol in front of a drunkard
You are counted as responsible
For his next misdeed
It is a form of ancient justice
That has not entirely reasserted itself
Here in the modern world

Shira

A shadowed dream I had a while back
Ended with the only thing I remember…
You
Somewhat disheveled
Shuffling slowly sideways by your living room table
Toward the room leading to your front door
You seemed to have just withstood a strong experience
Perhaps sexual…
I don't know

Your face looked sleepy
Or kinda burned out
Like people get waking up in the morning
After having had a salty meal for dinner the night before
Your dark hair was blown to the side and spooky
Like stuck that way
Weird and worrisome

I woke…
Why Shira, would I dream of you
When we aren't really intimates
Though the piece I wrote for you
I never tire of reading?

You are a love and a light
And a light and a love

And there aren't many people
Born as mystifying as the Moroccan Jewess

Be good to yourself, Shira
And if I have another dream of you
I'll be sure to let you know

— Maiche

My Nieces

My nieces
Sara and Eliza Schlein
Too smart to be reasoned with from the start
Candle-lit schtetl yentas
At holiday meals
When the dishes were pretty much half-cleared
Sometimes I'd find myself opposite these two
A five-year-old
A seven-year-old
We'd talk about the first grade
Or music classes
Or soccer
The girls go just as hard
Mia Hamm posters on the wall
And the Spice Girls…
And everything else that makes growing up in South Florida
    with two doctors for parents so abundantly free
These two…
To get them talking
My sister's tablecloth wiped of crumbs
In the dimmed brightness
There they sat and responded to my dumb queries
Tolerating me, really
I see their timeless Jewish beauty
Eliza

Some hieroglyphic that no pyramid wall could ever quite
get right
And Sarah…
The last golden loom's needle's point
Running straight down the center of her face

Forgive me…
They're my nieces
But if they were any more revealing of God's true spirit
The axis of the world would have to follow them around
Wherever they went
Sarah and Eliza
To get them talking…
These two…
My nieces

Forever 28

I'm going to go a bit further
In the name of dexterity
And all empty atheism
In the name of fighter jets hovering over the shimmering
    Mediterranean…
And new moon blood over the Black Sea

At Fifty

Did you ever get that notion
That at fifty
Things were supposed to get better?
Easier?
More sensible…?

Forget that shit!

Behavioral Despair

Behavioral Despair…
It wasn't so long ago I heard the term
My case opens and closes there
I've tried to shake it
But it's my rock bottom remainder
The ruins
The chisel and hammer
My excuse
My plea
My inmate number

Behavioral Despair
That's where it all went
Talk about something priceless poorly spent
The bread of sorrow
Bitter water
The highway of regret's disaster area

Behavioral Despair
Unto itself made manifest
Clowns are happy
Clowns are sad
Clowns are clowns
A frown is a smile turned upside down
Went to the show

Didn't rise from my seat
Didn't sing the songs on my way home
Didn't keep the ticket stub, nor the receipt
The dust of a plague seems to have my soul blown
Turned on the TV
Had to turn it off
Smoked my sixtieth cigarette
Began to cough
Love is something a thousand years ago in the air
A million miles away…
Milked
Bled
Stuffed
Drawn
Sculpted and portrayed

Behavioral Despair
There's an original thought out there
I could use it right now
People frame themselves in their own mess
People worship their loneliness
Like a prayer arrives to be spoken
Like a dream ends and you're awakened
To its continued emotion

Behavioral Despair
Truth is an arrow

And the gate is narrow that it passes through[10]
You do some sad, sad things baby
Oh, when it's you you're trying to lose[11]

Behavioral Despair
I will not condemn you
Nor get what I deny
I would ask the same of you
But failure would not die[12]

Behavioral Despair
A commencement documentary
Your very own voyeur's degree

Behavioral Despair
You're spoiling the mood
You're bringing us down
I'm a bluebird on a telegraph
Couldn't be more pleased or happy now

---

10 Dylan, Bob. "When He Returns." *Slow Train Comin'*
11 Springsteen, Bruce. "Living Proof." *Lucky Town.* A&M Records, 1992
12 Grateful Dead. "China Doll." *From the Mars Hotel,* 1974

Sabbatical

A sabbatical in … 1956
He's gone to find the meaning of God
"To find God," they say

She's taking a year off to "find herself"
So cliché
Passé

Anything but to stand before the Lord's throne with no
    love rising

Irish Saying

Life is brief

Things go wrong

May we always have enough

Your Daddy Loved You

Your Daddy loved you and he loved you full
Wouldn't you say that's what drove him?
A humility he found within
While coming to identify with the realms of our heritage
Baruch Hashem
The living oneness in our lives

I'm sure he must 've clowned around plenty
With the Russin kids when you were sprouting up
And I'm sure he kept after y'all
As though truly tending to sacred yield
He and Lynn
Together for so many months and years …

And you three
Each with distinctive voice
Brown-eyed and full of light
Julie
The first-born
Steel-willed and always so impossible
Peter
Once the shepherd, once the lamb
Elizabeth
The spark of your mother's shadow

You made them laugh forever
Both of them
And they loved you full
As your father sought spiritual connection
And its consecration in ceremonious prayer
So too should we be so vested
To find solace before our maker
Baruch Hashem

Wherever we are welcome is where we will be
This much we can relate to and believe
I thought I'd send the best words I could gather
In this time of your father's passing
Your family has always been a respected lot
May God bless and keep you always
Your daddy loved you full

— HDW

Twenty Earths

Twenty earths
Twenty earths with twenty creatures
All devoid of form
That evolved into twenty upright walking beings
Beings…
How many of these twenty beings on these twenty earths
Do you think quit their mess and straightened out
And made it through?

Upright…

Sadly II

Sadly, nice guys overdose, too

People think overdosing on heroin is a thing of toxicity
It's not
It's suffocation
The opiate numbs the area of the spinal cord
That sends involuntary messages to the pulmonary system
The lungs go to sleep and don't wake up

You're precious loved one is trashing a bathroom
Trying to *wake shit up*
And it ain't happenin'

She succumbs
All twisted
In a hideous, smothered snarl

Enter stretcher
"Who was she with?"
"Who did she belong to?"
"She was worth *what?*"
"And she gave it up to *these* ... this lot?"

Sadly, nice guys overdose, too.

Maybe God is…

Maybe God is all things just having found peace
And all things heading back into turbulence

What Do I Think of Orthodox Jews?

Orthodox Jewry
As they are raised up theocentrically
By the age of twenty
With their intellectual mechanism fully developed
They hold Genesis far away
Rolled up in the heavens
For mankind's redemption

To hurt one you would weep

Water Tower Bulb

A thousand-mile trip begins with the first step…
With this psyche?

Sharon Stuart

Sharon
The second time I approached you
Saying, "I love a woman with a wild beak"
I stepped back and noticed
There were children
Dancing behind your eyes
Laughing
And lighting up your face

She Shed

Look
TV...
Black people almost exclusively with black people
America, 2020
Y' never see it otherwise
Well-scrubbed black people with well-scrubbed black people
And how would that make you feel?

TV sucks anyhow
But this is waste
And a denial of cross-cultural beauty
The Germans love African beauty
And the French celebrate her

Sarah Spoke with Few Words

(Redheaded Publix Checkout Girl, Pensacola, Florida)

Sarah
I saw it
Your face is *music*

Bold
Steep
A dangerous slope to hold
Child…
Yours is the tune's breakdown
And before the day faded
I'd know it by heart

Sarah … I saw it … Your face is *music*

Muttering Bulletin Board

This just in…

I love it when you call me names

I have a tattoo of George Will on my body

What doth thou conceal

Oh great purveyor of truth and method?

You gotta watch what you say to a woman

And she's gotta watch what she does to a man

Have you read the aphid news?

I kept you in a place no one could touch

I kept you in my heart

Every once in a while

Veronica Hart comes across the screen

You can add to, but you can't take away

Me…?

I'm just as happy as the great Ben Vereen

Yes…

I'm a song and dance man after all

Yeah, Man ... Cool

No, I don't go around cool
And I don't think about having a million bucks
And whatever it is I'm covering up
I wish someone'd come tell me what it is
Whatever be it's vital importance...

You can go put a square root around something vast...

Catherine Keener

Five-hundred years would I know Catherine Keener
Five-hundred years would I hover and surround her in prayer
The soul that face houses
The winds in the wilds reach her by draw…
Forever

Now…
Five-hundred years is a long time
I imagine I wouldn't want to be an apparition for
    five centuries
Maybe I'll be her father in one life
And her mother in the next
Her boyfriend at the front door
Her girlfriend on the phone
God might make me her goldfish…
Or her dog
Her homeroom teacher
Her girl scout leader
Her next-door neighbor

It's just that her face is so noble and distinguished
So caring and feeling and knowing and…
Savage yet civilized
She's no Kathy

If I meet her in this life
The first thing I'll do is embrace her
And bury my nose in the folds of her neck
To greedily breathe in
Her natural sweet aroma

Minnie 'll be okay...
It's just me and you now, Catherine

Writer, Poet, Artist

What's the key to becoming a half-decent writer?
Giving a shit enough to get up and find a pen.

Please Step Out of the Vehicle

Those driving inebriated
Say, double the legal limit
Caught swerving and nodding out...
What should be done with them?
The United States does not practice corporal punishment
Though vehicular homicide is just under a capital offence
Mister "Dumbstruck-12-pack-Going-to-the-Store-for-More"
Didn't kill someone this time
But behind the wheel he grazed a rail
Crossed the lines
And swept the median a few times...

What do we do?
What is?
Revocation of license?
Yes
Time behind bars?
Yes, of course

But really...
With a repeat offender
Or even a first-time flagrant inebriant
Why not a few serious whacks before release?
I know, it's medieval
But that fucker wouldn't do it again...
Or throw their mother in jail with 'em

Maybe remove a finger...?
Something to remind the drunk
It was that finger that popped the top off the can
Oh, *then* he'll drink responsibly...
If he drinks at all
And not kill
Mow down your son or daughter
Or your wife on her way home
Or your folks out for a Sunday ride
Or *you*

Driving drunk is a *wickedness*

Stay at home, Chuck
Sober up, Mack
Oh God, Lucy
And Kevin...
You're not getting your keys till the sun comes up...
Tomorrow
Call an Über
Once you've vomited proper, ya'll

Whoredom

Whoredom…

Everybody wants some

Whoredom

World's oldest profession

A young one in a Halloween costume

Where might it begin?

Where might it end?

Dirty old man

Whoredom is as common as oxygen

Beware of what's too good to be true, son

Playwrights

Comedians

Musicians

Self-aggrandising politicians

Patriotism

A whore to power

A whore to passion

Little Boy Blue, he needed the money

Assume the position

Beware of enthusiasm

Breakin' even…

It don't feel like winnin'

It's said you judge a man

By his control over his passion

Whoredom
The circus boss kept a woman
It was like she *belonged* to him
Gone gamblin'
Gone whorin'
Seven deadly sins
When the fun begins
Cold hard cash
A fat man's grin

Whoredom
Can be a whore to provocation
To power
To access
To domination
To ruination
How is the snob the whore?
The snob always has something better
A snob's exaggeration
A snob's insinuation
Monopoly
Exclusivity
Until you want what the snob is dangling

Whoredom
The whore to mayhem
Terror
Chaos

What a whore lives for…
Sucker!
Whore!
If you keep calling me names
I won't come 'round here no more

Whoredom
Shiners don't require hospitalization
There are more than two ways
To drive yourself insane
I'd change my way of thinkin'…
If I could change my way of thinkin'
A better man
The Vatican
Amsterdam

Whoredom
People have to sell their daughters
For thin gruel in the morning
Makin' enemies
When there's no enemy of any kind
I've never been one who likes to trespass
But sometimes you just find yourself over the line[13]

Whoredom
Hi, baby … where you from?

---

13 Bob Dylan and Sam Shepard, "Brownesville Girl," *Knocked Out Loaded,* Colombia Records, 1986

Lookin' for some action?
Whoredom, an alternate income
I don't get that close to people
Does that answer your question?
What does Officer Friendly say to Mr. John?
Y' been serviced
Don't send me flowers, baby…
Tips are welcome

Whoredom

Beats workin'

Love is for poets and little tin women

True confessions

Variations

Forum

Xavier Hollander

Oh, I remember!

No kissin'

Jack and Jill went up the hill

Each with a quarter

Jill came down

With fifty cents…

Blushin'

Headed for the corner

Burning and Looting

Burning and looting must be fun
When you're from the ghetto
You know who "the man" is
The white world doesn't want you
Your black skin is "other" if not "less"
So any excuse to riot is…
Passionate
It's on!
Unifying
Come on!
Exciting
Great!
Finally
Again
Let's go!
Yeah
Bravery
Righteous
Damn Korean grocers!
Burning and looting
Reginald Denny
Fun
'92

This Kim

Hi, I'm Kim Kardashian
And unbelievably so
I've never been quite good enough for myself to stay as I am
If you do as I've done
You'll be widely admired
Wanted
Loved
Mentioned
Sought out
Adored
And popular
"Wanted" goes a long way

I'm from Armenia
I don't go back there much
They're religious
And who goes to church, anyway?

No worries
No regrets
My husband…
Yes, I have one
He gets attention on the ride of self-importance
Seriousness
Dangerousness

He doesn't sing
He just makes a lot of sense
Offers it to the masses
To the rest of us
The audience
My husband...
I've always loved his name
Kanye...
Kanye West
We are the original power couple outta Los Angeles

I'm Kim
There isn't a region of my body that hasn't gone under
   the knife
There's always someone around me with some more advice
What sense can be made of this life?

I even met the president of the United States
It was an *important* meeting
I wore a jacket
We spoke about prisons
Pardons
And clemency (which is a plea for mercy)
Lenience
Tolerance
There were cameras all around
The president was so nice

He said I could come back next year
We got along *famously*
I'm back in Catalina
(Which is off the coast of California)
People swim to Seal Beach annually…
(Once a year)
Why would they name it "Seal Beach?"
Seals are so … *ugly!*

Where are my sisters?
What are my ratings?
Who are *you?*
I need a drink!
What are my ratings?
I *hate* this color!
Does this make me look fat?
He's not supposed to wear a shirt when waxing my car!
Why do women have to have the babies?

This marriage thing…
Baby's mamas
Should we have made that tape?
I want a different masseuse
Is this a wrinkle?
Another wrinkle!
Why can't we always be beautiful…?
Young and beautiful?

Hot!
I wanna talk to Madonna

I wrote a song
It's called…

I Swear

In a millisecond of a dream
Everything around Conti toward Rampart
And another swath
Reaching Decatur was all gone

I'm not reporting this doomfully to scare anyone
Or manipulate…
Or am I?

The wine bottle
The Spanish kind
Sat on the synagogue's lower steps
Next to a flattened set of keys

"I want to be there but I can't"
"I'd like to have called"
"Make the mistake"
"Have you no empathy?"
"There were tears"
"What's this? I can't see you!"
"What am I doing here … for the umpteenth time?"
"Do something," she bade

There's action between brothers here
Her palm clutching white denim
Give me something!

I know you love me, Maiche
Salt!

"And I'm to take your place somewhere"

Maiche...
You're not just a thief
You're a creep!
Yeah...
Well, a few more of *those* just never came to be
What is it in that house
You think I'd need to take over anyhow?
(Key word: *need*)

Maybe it was Smadar I was supposed to love...
And not you
If I'd have been told that I'd spend thirty years like I have...
Yeah...
Maybe it *was* Smadar I was supposed to love
So many sad, sorry, bored, bland years ago

Song Written After Tires Slashed on Rickenbacker Causeway One Night

Do tongues cleave?

Does strength wither?

Do teeth shatter?

Do eyes dim?

Does hearing fade?

Do voices break?

Does skin crease?

Do souls sour?

Do wills die?

Are hopes dashed?

Do hearts fail?

Does blood thin?

Do tears flow?

Do prayers end?

A Thief

A thief thinks that the object he's taking
Was magically put there before him

Song for Kathleen Norris *(Acedia & Me)*

When nothing matters but the next laugh
When nothing matters but the next thrill...

There's a drugstore in the north star
But you're stuck on the moon
There's a hospital on Venus
But you're bedridden on Mars
There's a music store on Mercury
But you're two cents flat on Pluto
There's a shoe repair on Saturn
But you're tripping in the sun
There's a prayer book on Earth...

After a Good Cry

After a good cry
The earth has stopped spinning in the sky
After a good cry
You're beyond the reasons why
You're human again
You are your own best friend
Doesn't happen often
That day I went t' crying
There was no denying

After a good cry
Life is the same but knots are untied
It just comes over you
Sometimes you need to cry
Y' never knew y' had it in you
Up until…
You lose grip on your heart
And your mind surrenders its will

When you're a kid
You cry the day your dog dies
In this dirty world
You cry when your mother meets her earthly demise
Alone in a kitchen
No one 'round to listen
Awash in the will

I have a heart after all…
I could've slumped into a pile
After a good cry
Only what's worthwhile is worthwhile

Anything perverse is a stick in the eye
After a good cry
You've just come from
Where words don't apply
What's been mounting … comes
Walls are breached
A river runs

After a good cry…
If I could just hear my mother's voice
Funny…
It comes in dreams
When we have less a world of choice
If I could just hear my father call my name
Underneath, weren't we so much the same?

After a good cry
You know nothing that hurts gonna last forever
All my cunning
Always so right
So original
Clever

After a good cry
Chains been *shocked*
Like a prison break
A weight's been dropped
Yes, child
You've lived with a heavy mistake

After a good cry
The water
The ground
The sky
Tears are what's left
Those truths arrived
I see again your laughing crescent eyes
Even if it does
Love never dies
I stood still with tears running hot down my face
Was I trembling?
Weeping?
My chest was heaving
Alone in a familiar place

After a good cry
Life relents
You're helpless
Helpless
Somewhere in there you make a wish

After a good cry
Human again
First time flying
First time landing
I was your Dom
You were my Catherine
On a train with Charlie Chaplin
After a good cry
The dawning of understanding
So long in the whirlwinds
Now I'm in some better place
Now I'm in some better standing
After a good cry

Financial District at Dawn Shot
(from *Gumball Rally*)

I think I may be the Gary Bussey of soft rock

> *Roll on, yellow Camaro*
> *Yellow Camaro, roll on*
> *A-roll-on-I-say*
> *Roll on, yellow Camaro*
> *Yellow Camaro, roll on*

Roll on!

One Christmas

One Christmas
I wandered into the Stephen Talkhouse on
   Washington Avenue
This Miami band called "The Goods" was playing tight
   and loud
I got a beer and sat near a large well-lit Christmas tree
There weren't that many people in the place
Then the band went into the Kinks' song
"Father Christmas"
The Gibson guitars and the stalk of bells got me *goin'*
And I got it in my head
That I was gonna go tackle that Christmas tree
Just to show the band what they were doin' to me

My pulse shot up
Am I gonna do this?
I'd gotten in some trouble with several of the managers there
For rockin' out too hard
Sitting there
With that song in my ears
I was a step away from some sort of rock 'n' roll glory
I was either gonna get electrocuted
Or get my ass kicked

It would have been fun…
But I pussied out

Father Christmas, give us the money
Don't mess around with those silly toys
We'll beat you up if you don't hand it over
We want your bread so don't make us annoyed
Give all the toys to the little rich boys[14]

---

14 "Misfits." The Kinks. Arista Records, 1977

I'm Thinkin'

I'm thinkin' I'll go drinkin'
Grade my papers over a nice cold beer
I'm thinkin' I'll go drinkin'
Hijack the jukebox
Play the B-sides y' never hear

I don't get behind the wheel drunk
Don't know anyone who does
You've got to be one absolutely stupid sonofabitch
To drive wasted, punk

Twenty-million teenagers with no concept of time
Speed and distance
Radio
Telephone
Coffee cup
'Zup?
Stems
Seeds
Oncoming traffic
Statistics
Texting
Kids

What am I doin' in this bar?
"What are you always here writin' about?"

I'm a teacher
I mark and correct
Well,Teach
Let me buy you a stout
Why not?
I'm almost done
And it's early yet

I can drink you under the table
Daddy used to run moonshine
Really ... I'm a complete lightweight
A couple o' beers and I'm disabled
I guess it was great fun to me
Once upon a time

　　When Jones' Ale was new, my boy
　　When Olsen's Ale we brewed...

I'm Teach...
Let me tell you...
When I passed through Chicago for the first time
I needed a steady line of something
To get my blood back to red from blue

In some countries
In some cultures
The consumption of alcohol is frowned upon

It must be something important to them
They're sure missin' out on all this rock 'n' roll fun

Y' gonna buy one or be one?

Last call, people

You alright to drive, Kevin?
Kevin?
Kevin!

Bartender…
Susan…
Sooooo-san…
Give me my keys, woman!

All the King's Men (the other one)

Sometimes a man can want something so bad...

He's so full of *want*

He plain forgets what it *is* he wants

Sister in Time

My sister in time
All the other kids wait there in line
She and I tap shoulders and dance through like its fine
Those two…

My sister in time
Beyond the first day of summer
We don't acknowledge one other
Till Christmas time
We might as well be on different continents

My sister in time
When it starts raining
She drags me outta my room
Little brother
Big sister
Lightning strike
Thunder boom
She's on fire
It's raining
From my sister in time
I learned the futility of complaining

My sister in time
In living color

Black and white
We were latchkey kids, alright
She gave the neighbor boy a kiss on the mouth
When Becky slept over
She left crying without her socks

My sister in time
Left me at home
Stole my bike
Billy played a Lynyrd Skynyrd song on the guitar
Started selling little baggies
And bought herself a big ol' car
An Oldsmobile
Seventy-four
Big and green

Everywhere she goes
It's enough to break hearts
Someone always gets hurt
A fire always starts[15]
No one hates failure more than she
There's no one who could care less
She's otherworldly
A c-a-t-a-s-t-r-o-p-h-e

To think that the same blood runs in our veins...

---

15 Bob Dylan and Carole Bayer Sager, "Under Your Spell" Columbia Records, 1986

My sister in time
Maybe you have one
So wild and sharp
She knows everything about me
She knows you're afraid of the dark

I didn't mention…
She always keeps an apple in her purse
When she takes a bite
The juice runs down her chin
My sister in time

My sister in time
She's not insecure
She lets on
A clown's clown, really
Never knows when to stop
Once she gets silly
She's a Libra in the house of Leo
We were born on the same day
Ten-thousand years ago
My sister in time

Cami
Are you still going through men like paper towels?
I'm in Breckenridge
I think of you sometimes
Yes, Cami

When the wolves howl

Cami
A woman so wild
Is not to be tamed

Cami
Is the thrill of the stars
Still your middle name?

Concerts of My Youth II

Warren Zevon

Me and my Junior High School friend, Sean Edelson, and his "Pops," Arthur, were excited to greet one another on the hardwood floor in front of the stage, pre-show, very underage at a bar on the Fort Lauderdale Strip, "Summers on the Beach." No frills; just songs. Black Ovation guitars, his favorites through the years. Jerry Douglas played pedal steel that night.

Zevon's baritone *let me in.*

My other buddy, Joel Schantz, has got a picture: One arm's around Warren and the other is raised in "Yeah!" Zevon's laughing next to him.

I could sing all of his stuff as a teen, and I did on many an afternoon in my room with the door shut.

Of the songs I sing acapella, his are automatic go-tos.

"Studebaker" — *Left my home in Monterey...*

"Under the Eaves" — *I was sitting in the Hollywood Hawaiian Hotel...*

"French Inhaler" — *How y' gonna make your way in the world, woman...?*

"Mohammed's Radio" — *Everybody's restless...*

Warren Zevon...

Somethin' else

I'd like to make note that Joel and Sean are both "lifers." They have carried through their rock 'n' roll dreams brick-by-brick. Joel is like one of Rick Neilsen's beautiful, bald-headed nephews, about to pounce. And Sean's musical dexterity can charm the pants off the prettiest girl in the room. Really ... I've seen it. I love them both and wish them well.

Elvis Costello comes out and says, "I've been watching TV for five days; anything can happen."

His drummer set the kit down low, kept his sound sorta *punchin'*.

I ran into Andy Zaron, another childhood friend, at Sunrise. Elvis played a Fender telecaster all night. I don't remember what shade.

The Who

Midstate Tampa Stadium, The Tangerine Bowl, with the very musical Edelson family again. We also went up there to see the Stones around that time. I don't recall too much of the show. I think Van Halen warmed up. Through the binoculars handed to me by Sean's father, Arthur, I could see Pete Townsend's and John Entwistle's Hi-Watt amps and Pete's numbered Gibson guitars.

We had all their records. The Who fed us rare bolts of power. The whole world has always wanted to grab hold of Roger Daltry's locks and "join together with the band."

And y' know, right now, Pete and Roger, the surviving members, could make a few calls and be playing to 750,000 people in Rio tomorrow.

Marshall Tucker Band

Portland Civic Center. Camp Samoset night out from Casco, Maine. Eleven years old. I sat with Scotty Davis and Sammy Seder. Some band named Frankie Goes to Hollywood had a song on the radio; they warmed up. Then those boys came out with their tobacco voices and their best Levi's and boots.

"Can't Ya See?"

"Amy, What You Gonna Do?"

Both *happened*.

I'm sure the volume was satisfying. The concert experience was born to me.

(Frankie Goes to Hollywood. I can't believe I fucking remember that!)

Chuck Mangione

My very first show—at Miami Beach Theatre of the Performing Arts.

"Feels So Good" was top of the charts The world slowed down for a while with that tune—not your typical Y100 FM radio fare. We were tamed and then lifted. I begged my parents to go. They sent me with my big sister Debbie who was in the tenth grade. She wore a burgundy, paisley top and earth shoes. I couldn't believe a theater could be so luxurious—thousands of seats all covered in fine, maroon fabric.

We sat near the soundboard, blessed by Chuck's cultured flügelhorn.

Grant Geissner's extraordinary guitar solo!

"Children of Sanchez" playing through an adobe village
I think the drummer might have had four arms!

Southside Johnny and the Asbury Jukes
"Yes it is!"

Nervous at the door of the Agora Ballroom — *way back*

I don't remember who drove us there, but I do remember a lot of guys with brass horns blowin' on a small stage.

Joan Baez

Somewhere in west Fort Lauderdale, 1985

The whole show took place under threatening skies. "We Beat the Rain," she said.

What a quiet soul commanding such a stellar voice that Spanish body holds.

Brian Setzer

Dressed in green with a whole half-an-orchestra blowin' behind him, Lionel Hampton-style.

Double bass drummer.

Poppin' the big beat

Brian looked like a prize-fighter.

Made me think of the rigors of the road.

Joan Jett

In her standard black Converse with black Gibson, **Joan Jett and the Blackhearts** at the Agora Ballroom. MTV was raging, and here was its bad girl, six feet away.

And I don't care what it sounds like, but Gary Ryan, the bass player, was so good looking I couldn't take my eyes off him.

But when I did, there was Joan Jett layin' down some power chords. "Yeah. Oh yeah."

Shawn Colvin

Holding her own with just a guitar and her voice, at the Eden Roc hotel in Miami Beach.

Forty-five minutes of brandywine.

She can show *you* how it's done.

Heart

At the Miami Arena in the handicapped section with Miami Beach Senior High School Music program and director Doug Burris. Burris regarded Heart as the masses did—unstoppable iron dames surrounded by killers.

A show like that goes by like a coupe, a tryst, a skirmish, a riot.

The girls' big voices.

Flat-out drumming.

Guitarists who have to play as demandingly as they did when they were twenty and hungry.

Heart: FM radio right in your face.

Crosby, Stills, and Nash

I saw them at the Miami-Knight center in the late 80s. They had the same fire. I know where David Crosby was stepping on the stage when they played "The Last Whale."

Their performance at Live Aid in the noonday sun was *epic*.

Lone Justice

June, 1985. Maria McKee had a city boy on drums, a Texas highway guitarist, and a rockabilly bass player behind her. There I stood by a small stage in Boston, listening to their hot premiere record. Cowpunk was born. Peter Wolf, lead singer of the J. Geils Band was at the bar, and I swear he was glowing. Really; the cat was *glowing*.

Chuck Berry

Sunrise. He was the blood, a power-paw. He seemed dissatisfied with his backing band. He was in his early sixties then, I guess, and still rockin'. His fingers as big as corn dogs.

The times that man must have known.

I wonder if they buried him with his Gibson ES-355.

Seraphic Fire

A treasure in sound. Something you can give yourself to entirely. And South Florida's own.

Neil Sedaka

In white and red with a nine-foot white grand piano, at the Youth Fair in '77.

Walking along country roads with my baby.

It starts to rain; it begins to pour.

The crowd roars.

Wow! FM Love.

He was half-bald in lapels, but he rocked it.

Fushu Daiko

Japanese big drums. Pompano, Florida. If I could do it again, I'd bring psilocybin. I was almost killed on the way in by a speeding driver in the opposite lane. If you can remember the Mitsubushi commercial, that's Fushu Daiko. They don't boogie but they do sweat.

Mark Knopfler

"Golden Heart," his first solo effort after Dire Straits was the beginning of something solid. I saw him in Miami Beach. To have his records is to be *wealthy*. You can say that about a lot of the arts, but Mark Knopfler plays lead electric guitar without a pick—and no one else does it quite like him.

The Eleanor McMain High School Gospel Choir

The school that Mahalia Jackson built.

At JazzFest '07, it's real hot. I'm kinda dry. I smoke some regs at the side of the tent. I make my way in and I find a seat. It's much cooler.

Suddenly the stage fills with a choir of black children descending in age from high school seniors to sixth graders. Six rows of seats. Probably sixty kids, all with clean tee-shirts on and dark sunglasses—the Blues Brothers type. The heavyset conductor takes the platform, says something to the crowd, turns around, and begins to use those voices like his own philharmonic orchestra.

I sat in my chair and had to raise my arms several times in adulation.

JazzFest. So what do you do in late April?

After the performance, I walked up to the stage and asked if I could have the poster in the display. I still have it.

Lucinda Williams

Also at JazzFest '07. The road had her a little croaky, but Lucinda owned it all before the first song. We love her like we love John Prine — an authority with teardrops.

Lucinda has her own way of singing — traditional yet always original. Her conscience rejects caricature and formula. There's something vital and important in each of her songs. As a songwriter she's not accusatory or petulant — worn-out qualities found in all forms of popular music.

Listen … you write about who you're hanging with, and she respects her companions. Those are the best songs — redemption, not war. And with a name like Lucinda… Unforgettable.

Eric Burdon and The Animals

In Tel Aviv. I was fifteen and stupid. Me and my buddies met the band and I told them they were better than they were way back when. One of the guys turned and said in full English accent, "I certainly hope so." They played their MTV hit, "The Night Keeps Movin' On."

U2

At Joe Robbie Stadium.

They've always been just the best thing in the wind.

And on the ground with ninety-six 18-wheelers full of gear.

Roger Waters

The Pros and Cons of Hitchhiking. Lakeland, Florida, '84. I kid-napped my girlfriend and we rode up there. By the time we got back, I felt like a deranged sociopath.

World-class rock 'n' roll.

Bill Monroe and the Bluegrass Boys

At the Bottom Line in New York City. Bluegrass! Bluegrass runs. Harmony's high lonesome. Bluegrass's best in the city tonight! Mandolins and dreadnought guitars. Bill Monroe in a white Stetson hat. He brought Tennessee with him!

The Radiators, The Nevilles, Ladysmith Black Mambazo, Dr. John

Bonnie Raitt

John Prine

Steve Forbert

The Red Clay Ramblers

Natural Causes

Gordon Lightfoot

Ofra Haza

Aley Scheer

The Gypsy Kings

Great Beatles tribute bands

Lyle Lovett

G.E. Smith

Stevie Ray Vaughan

Amy Mann

Prince

Steve Earle

The Wallflowers

The Notting Hillbillies

Emmylou Harris

The Waterboys

The Rain Dogs

The Iron City House Rockers

The Great Peter Betan

And a whole lot more!

DETROIT! HOW Y' FEELIN!?

Done to Y' Things

I guess it would have to have done things to y'…
Done to y' things
Yes, I guess it would have to have done things to y'…
Done to y' things

I wonder who you were
How you were as a child
She's a little, little kid
But not a toddler
Arms folded
Chin down
Lower lip pursed
Her brown eyes trained
On whatever's going on around her
Laughing
Smiling
Never one of the girls
And boys just seem so stupid!
Thick brown hair
Parted in the center
Long braids

Your mama couldn't have warned you
About a lot of what you've found
Once…

Twice…
Three times you're out
Batter has to go back and sit down

You don't have to be my girl
You don't have to be his girl
You can always be your own girl[16]

You need *me* to tell you to look around?

And there's that little kid
Hands on her hips
In a big house
Which child's voice makes the deepest sound?

---

16 Jakob Dylan, *Be Your Own Girl,* "The Wallflowers,"
Virgin Records, 1992

Get It On

Got my gutbucket blues daddy out
My Sun House stomp
Got my *yaawp*
Hear my *yaawp!*
Got my J.T. and my Stephen Bishop
I'm whistlin' Dixie swingin' a broom
Pushin' a mop...
When I play my harmonica
My hound dog howls and will not stop

REO Speedwagon...
That's the ticket!
Shut up!

Turn it up!
I got my yodel
Any parking lot is my mountaintop...

Aye, Calypso, the places you've been to
The things that you've shown us
The stories you tell

Aye, Calypso, I sing to your spirit
The men who have served you
So long and so well...[17]

---

17 Denver, John. "Calypso." RCA Records, 1975

A SHIP *of War, of the third Rate With Rigging &c. at Anchor.*

Ghost Ship

She was a ghost ship alright
Absent of captain and crew
Born to dawn's cloud over deep water
Her deck told tales of skirmish
The vessel…
One of the Lord's own toys
Dragged through time
His blanket
The surface of the seas

A ghost ship
To salt and wind and rain
Her hard, heavy planks
Cut and carted to barge past the Great Rock
Offshore to the British isles
Lofted, laid, and launched
Christened H.M.S *Deliverance*
Cornwall, 1783

The Upright Walking Creature

The Book of Revelations is a distillation
Of all that comes before it
From Genesis onward
It was written
By either a Nostradamus-type figure
Who had grown tired of always *getting* it
Or maybe by some committee…
A tribunal of rabbis
Dispelling all the superstitions of their troubled times

A distillation…
Hollywood aims at sensationalizing
What is in fact quite plain
All the monsters and fire mentioned in its pages
Are man's ongoing, murderous blunder

If the golden rule
Is to do unto to others as you would have them do unto you…
All the conundrum in our contradiction…
How much trouble we make for ourselves…
Temptation's not an easy thing
Some say we have no choice
That it runs in our veins

The upright walking creature

The Burst Out Awards

It's like I want to go running down a hill
Or burst out in dance in the street
When I hear The Beatles' "Lovely Rita, Meter Maid"
It is as if a thousand spears *warp*
From note one
The piano so affectionately *there*
Watering with cool pillars of blue ice
And that's not a jug band for a bassline
It's an Indian drum that George Martin tolerated
And expertly exploited
As only George Martin could
With only four tracks at his disposal
And four spry, ruddy lads in London Town, '67
Lovely Rita

And John Lennon's "Mind Games"
A light coming on in a darkness you did not know held you
A little stick figure at a microphone
Suddenly illuminates the universe
Makes me want to burst out in song and dance away forever

And we must always be reminded of how long it has been
Since we last heard "While My Guitar Gently Weeps"
Prince's guitar work at George Harrison's induction…

Bursting out!

God Bless Noam Chomsky

He'll probably live to 103
But when Noam Chomsky passes on
I'll go to the entrance to the cemetary
Holding a sign with the words:

"He had no equal!"

Deliverance

Blind Jesus

Deaf Jesus

Scarred Jesus

Starved Jesus

Jesus risen

Limping Jesus

Weeping Jesus

Bleeding Jesus

Jesus whipped

Slaving Jesus

Holy Jesus

Beautiful Jesus

Silent Jesus

Robed jesus

Crowned Jesus

Praised Jesus

King Jesus

Brother Jesus

Baby Jesus

Father Jesus

Merciful Jesus

Got a friend in Jesus

Forgiving Jesus

The rod of Jesus

The terrible swift sword of Jesus

My Jesus

Your Jesus

Too many people have lied in the name of Jesus to hear
    the call

The Lord Jesus

The victory of Jesus

Healing Jesus

Gracious Jesus

The love of Jesus

Jesus on the main line

Tell Him what you want

Jesus is real to me

That is why I love him so

Jesus doesn't like sin

Pressing on with Jesus

Jesus, I'd hate to be you on that day

Jesus the heart fixer

Jesus the mind regulator

True till the end, Jesus

Unforgettable Jesus

Jesus with the woman at the well

"I pity you for your weakness," said Jesus

Jesus, y' gotta watch what you say to a woman

Jesus, I got the impossible done

Jesus, the white man loved an Indian maiden

But with notions his canoe was laden

Jesus makes beauty from ugly things

Jesus walked as a rastaman

Jesus, so many people doubt him

I can't live without him

Gone the distance with Jesus

Try to be good with Jesus

The sins of the fathers unto the third generation

Jesus, may your mistakes be your own

By whom was he chastised?

By whom was he hated…?

Verily I say unto you

"Your sin will find you out"

The ghetto you build is the one you end up in

Let the guiltless cast the first stone

Jesus, consider her jewels

Jesus in modern times

As ice or as fire

Never lukewarm

Love and theft and Jesus

We did love each other more than we'd ever tell

Help me now, Jesus

Other Books by Maiche Lev

Speaking Circus
Lights Down
Floored
Still Life - With Extras
Deadlock Backdraft: Above the Elecric Gardens
On the Moon You Sharpen Stone
Busy Murals